10 Hacks For Citrix NetScaler ADC/MPX/SDX

NETSCALER
HACKS

Extend the life of this hardware with amazing ideas for legacy
Citrix NetScaler/ADC/MPX/SDX hardware.

By Joseph Moses / Bonsai Entertainment Publishing

NetScaler Hacks - Table of Contents

COPYRIGHT

BONSAI ENTERTAINMENT PUBLISHING PRESENTS:

Understanding the
NetScaler SDX

The Story Of How I Built My Own SDX Clone and How You Can Too.

BY JOSEPH MOSES

DEDICATION

This book is dedicated to:

Our Lord Jesus Christ

My wife and kids

The Citrix NetScaler Development Team

Roy S. - My friend who encouraged me to write my first book

Everyone who has supported my work by buying a copy of my books!

FORWARD

Before we get started, I want to give you a big "**THANK YOU**" for buying this book or eBook and spending some time with me. I sincerely hope you will enjoy the ideas I have come up. More importantly, I hope you will take some of these ideas and implement them yourself. I look forward to hearing about what you have done and learn about your new ideas for legacy NetScaler hardware!

Now, lets get started!

The Citrix NetScaler, now know as Citrix ADC is a family of Application Delivery Controllers (ADC). They are purpose-built appliances dedicated to doing a lot of really cool things in the data center.

However, when you get right down to it, they are just computers. More exactly, they are servers that run the Citrix NetScaler firmware / operating system that allows it to do these really cool things.

As these machines age, they are deemed to be at their End Of Life (EOL) and are no longer officially supported by Citrix. As a result they are often found on eBay and other sites for sale at very reasonable prices.

The unique thing about the Citrix ADC is that unlike commodity servers from companies like HP, DELL or Lenovo, the community of IT experts who understand the Citrix ADC is rather limited. Thus, there may not be much competition for legacy NetScaler hardware on the auction sites.

My Lab Data Center

In addition, once you have 1 or even 2 NetScalers for your lab, most people feel like that is enough. But not me.

While this book is dedicated to older or "legacy" NetScaler appliances, much of what I discuss can be applied to any other similar server hardware be they old or new.

Everything you read about in "**NetScaler Hacks**" I have personally done and researched. I have spent countless hours reading, building and hacking my legacy NetScalers. I hope the information in this book will be valuable to you and will allow you to breath new life, into your legacy NetScaler hardware!

Finally, for obvious and legal reasons; the information contained in this book, "NetScaler Hacks", is for EDUCATIONAL PURPOSES ONLY and YOU ALONE will be responsible for any damage you do to your hardware or systems that you attempt to modify, change or enhance.

## Chapter 1

INTRODUCTION

What Is A Legacy NetScaler? Any NetScaler Past The Citrix Defined EOL (End Of Life) Date Or Potentially Any NetScaler Past The Refresh Time Of The Customer.

NetScaler 7000 - EOL 2013

NetScaler MPX 5500/7500/10500 - EOL 2018

NetScaler MPX/SDX 8200 - EOL 1/1/2024

NetScaler MPX/SDX 11500 - EOL 12/31/2019

"Citrix NetScaler" becomes "Citrix Application Delivery Controller" (ADC)

Recently, Citrix rebranded all their NetScaler appliances to "Citrix ADC" meaning "Citrix Application Delivery Controller". I will refer to these appliances as either NetScaler or ADC or by their model number where required.

 If you are reading this book **"NetScaler Hacks"**, you probably have a legacy Citrix NetScaler or a similar "purpose built appliance" and are looking for ideas of what to do with this hardware. Usually, there is absolutely nothing wrong with the hardware you possess, it is just that the appliance maker has decided to no longer officially support it. Or, the original purchaser of the appliance; usually a large corporation, has already depreciated the cost of the appliance and needs to upgrade their hardware according to their upgrade/refresh cycle.

 These legacy appliances are available on eBay and other auction sites, usually for very affordable prices. The older models are usually under $100 and the less old models can be had for about $200 each.

As of the writing of this book, early 2020, I have purchased the MPX/SDX 8200 on eBay for as little as $49. Most recently, I have acquired several MPX/SDX 11500's for the average price of just under $200 each. Both prices included free shipping within the USA.

The MPX/SDX 8200 has not yet have reached EOL. It runs a very powerful 3.4GHz 4-Core XEON E1275 processor with hyper-threading yielding 8-threads, and comes with 32GB RAM. It runs very quiet (almost no fan noise) and it is available on eBay from time to time.

This book is dedicated to providing support for all of these legacy appliances. Some of these ideas may resonate with you, others will not apply. I look forward to finding out what you do with your legacy hardware!

UNIVERSAL UPGRADES

There are some common upgrades you can make to improve the performance or usability of your legacy NetScaler appliances. These are all very easy and either free or relatively cheap to do.

GET VIDEO- EXPOSING the front VIDEO PORT - for security

reasons, the video ports on all NetScalers are covered up. However, with a Dremel-like rotary tool you can easily remove this plastic cover to provide access to the built in video.

GET USB - EXPOSING the front USB PORT(s) - again for security reasons the USB ports on the front of all NetScalers are covered up. Again using a Dremel-like rotary tool you can remove the plastic that covers these ports and give yourself access.

MAKE QUIET (part A)- Change to 4-pin PWM fans - If your NetScaler comes with 3-pin fans they will be loud. You can easily find 4-pin replacement fans on eBay and replace them. After that, you can go into the BIOS (press Delete key during boot) and change the fan speed to "4-pin server". This will drastically reduce the noise that these appliances make.

GET QUIET (part B)- Change FAN BIOS settings - on newer NetScalers that have 4-pin fans they are usually set at the factory to run at full speed. These appliances just require a change in the BIOS to "LOW POWER, LOW NOISE" setting. Do the same to your older NetScaler after you have changed the internal cooling fans to 4-pin PWM versions.

Upgrade Memory - The X7DCU based NetScalers can support up to 48-GB RAM. The X8DTE based NetScaler can support up to 192GB RAM.

Enable the SATA ports - From the factory all NetScalers have their SATA ports disabled. Going into the BIOS and enabling these will allow you to connect and use your SATA drives in your NetScaler.

## Chapter 2

NETSCALER AS A SWITCH/FIREWALL

The NetScaler Is A Switch If Layer 3 Is Enabled And A Bridge If Layer 2 Is Enabled

One option is to keep the NetScaler as a dedicated switch

You can continue to run the NetScaler firmware or

Run another firmware like VyOS or pfSense

Depending on your use case, you may want to keep the legacy NetScaler as either a dedicated simple switch or even as an intelligent switch. Whether you decide to continue to run the NetScaler firmware may be dependent on having a valid license for the functionality you seek to deploy.

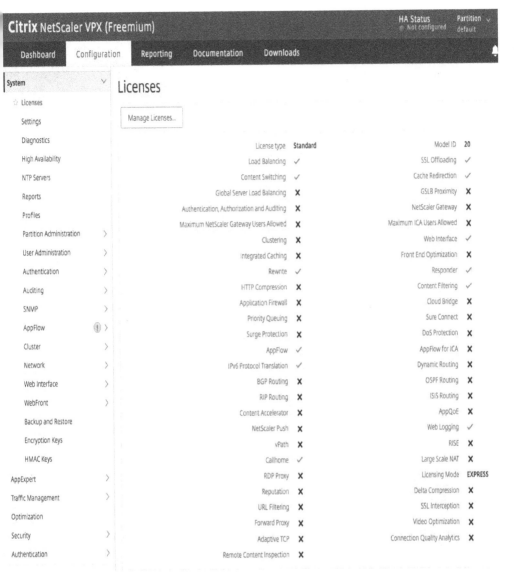

System

- Licenses
- Settings
- Diagnostics
- High Availability
- NTP Servers
- Reports
- Profiles
- Partition Administration >
- User Administration >
- Authentication >
- Auditing >
- SNMP >
- AppFlow >
- Cluster >
- Network >
- Web Interface >
- WebFront >
- Backup and Restore
- Encryption Keys
- HMAC Keys

AppExpert >
Traffic Management >
Optimization
Security >
Authentication >

Licenses

Manage Licenses...

License type	**Standard**	Model ID	**20**
Load Balancing	✓	SSL Offloading	✓
Content Switching	✓	Cache Redirection	✓
Global Server Load Balancing	✗	GSLB Proximity	✗
Authentication, Authorization and Auditing	✗	NetScaler Gateway	✗
Maximum NetScaler Gateway Users Allowed	✗	Maximum ICA Users Allowed	✗
Clustering	✗	Web Interface	✓
Integrated Caching	✗	Front End Optimization	✗
Rewrite	✓	Responder	✓
HTTP Compression	✗	Content Filtering	✓
Application Firewall	✗	Cloud Bridge	✗
Priority Queuing	✗	Sure Connect	✗
Surge Protection	✗	DoS Protection	✗
AppFlow	✓	AppFlow for ICA	✗
IPv6 Protocol Translation	✓	Dynamic Routing	✗
BGP Routing	✗	OSPF Routing	✗
RIP Routing	✗	ISIS Routing	✗
Content Accelerator	✗	AppQoE	✗
NetScaler Push	✗	Web Logging	✓
vPath	✗	RISE	✗
Callhome	✓	Large Scale NAT	✗
RDP Proxy	✗	Licensing Mode	**EXPRESS**
Reputation	✗	Delta Compression	✗
URL Filtering	✗	SSL Interception	✗
Forward Proxy	✗	Video Optimization	✗
Adaptive TCP	✗	Connection Quality Analytics	✗
Remote Content Inspection	✗		

But, for example Layer 2 mode / Layer 3 switching functionality should work just fine without any valid license or an expired license or Freemium version.

Citrix NetScaler VPX (Freemium)

Dashboard | Configuration | Reporting | Do

⊖ Configure Modes

☑ Fast Ramp   ☐ Layer 2 Mode

☐ Use Source IP   ☐ Client side Keep Alive

☐ TCP Buffering   ☐ MAC based forwarding

☑ Edge Configuration   ☑ Use Subnet IP

☑ Layer 3 Mode (IP Forwarding)   ☑ Path MTU Discovery

☐ Static Route Advertisement   ☐ Direct Route Advertisement

☐ Intranet Route Advertisement   ☐ IPv6 Static Route Advertisement

☐ IPv6 Direct Route Advertisement   ☐ Bridge BPDUs

☐ Media Classification   ☐ ULFD

OK | Close

For the smaller appliances it might make sense to use them as a dedicated switch. But for the more powerful appliances it may seems like a waste of resources.

Lets look at the various models and discuss some of the possibilities.

NETSCALER 7000 AS SWITCH

NS 7000 front

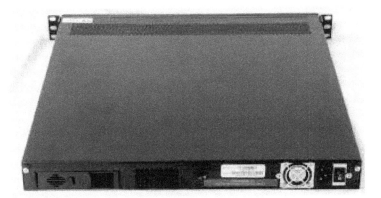

NS 7000 rear

Released in 2008, the NetScaler 7000 is an Intel Pentium-4 based appliance with Eight (8)-1Gb RJ45 ports and a serial console port on the front. It the rear, it sports a Compact Flash (CF) card reader, a 3.5" SATA drive bay, a USB 2.0 port and the power connector.

The NetScaler 7000 went EOL in 2013, but it could continue to work as a NetScaler 7000 if you have a non-expired license.

----

*Please contact me if you happen to have a *any* non-expiring license for the NetScaler 7000, I'll trade you a N90X mug for that!

contact me: admin@n90x.info

The NetScaler 7000 can run NetScaler Firmware up to version 9.2 CL (single core). It's relatively quiet to operate and uses the least amount of power of the NetScalers we will discuss.

VyOS (open source switch software) or **pfSense** (open source firewall) can be installed on this hardware and redeployed as a new network device in your lab or data center.

Open Source LINKS:

VyOS: https://www.vyos.io

pfSense: https://www.pfsense.org

Citrix no longer hosts NetScaler 7000 firmware on their website. As a service to my readers, I will post a 9.2 CL image that you can restore to a CF card on my website https://www.N90X.info.

NETSCALER MPX 5500/7500/10500 AS SWITCH

MPX 5500 - 1U

MPX 7500 - 1U

MPX 10500 - 2U

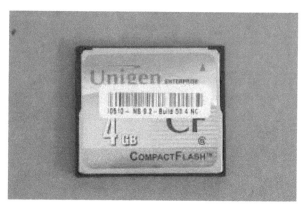

4 GB CF card

I have grouped these 3 NetScaler models together because they all share the same motherboard; the Supermicro X7DCU. They differ only by BIOS settings, CPU(s), memory amount, type / number of network ports and case size.

Without any changes, any of these models would make a fine switch or firewall running the **NetScaler** Firmware, **VyOS** or **pfSense**. You will be able to utilize all the existing ports in such configurations. In Chapter 7, we will look at upgrading some of these models to a 10 Gb switch.

NETSCALER MPX/SDX 11500 AS SWITCH

The NetScaler MPX/SDX 11500 is a very powerful Dual Hex (six) core server (so 12 cores, 24 threads) with 48 GB RAM standard (upgradeable to 192 GB RAM). It comes with 4 x 10 Gb SFP+ ports and 8 x 1 Gb SFP or RJ45 ports.

This powerful server can do a lot of things simultaneously. It could still run as a NetScaler ADC in your environment or as a switch / firewall running the 3rd party software discussed previously. However, it's best use case is in virtualization or as a dedicated server. We will cover these topics in the Chapter 3 "NetScaler as Dedicated Server" and in Chapter 4 "NetScaler as a Virtualization platform"

NETSCALER AS A DEDICATED SERVER

NETSCALER 11500 (TOP) NETSCALER 10500 (BOTTOM) WITH FACE

PLATES REMOVED

Legacy NetScaler MPX 5500, MPX 7500, MPX 10500

Upgradeable to Dual Quad Core Intel XEONs

Upgradeable to 48 GB RAM

Upgradable to 6 SATA II drives

Built in Video (hidden) support by all server operating systems

If you have the older MPX 5500/7500/10500 hardware you can use them as a dedicated server. They are quite powerful and upgradable and can be put to use as dedicated servers, for example:

Linux / Windows / Web Servers

NAS / FreeNAS servers

Dedicated DB Servers

Dedicated Workstation

If you have the MPX 11500 you can upgrade the memory from 48GB (factory shipped) to 192GB. You can add up to 6 SATA III hard drives to the built in rear drive bays, 2 x 3.5" drives and 4 x 2.5" drives.

Really, these are just servers and can be deployed in any server capacity you can imagine.

X7DCU MOTHERBOARD - MPX
5500/7500/10500

The MPX 5500/7500/10500 all use the Supermicro X7-DCU motherboard

The Original MPX 5500/7500/10500 series of Citrix NetScalers all share the same Supermicro X7-DCU motherboard. They are highly upgradable and are still considerably powerful considering their age.

The MPX 5500 has a single XEON E5205 processor with 2 cores.

The MPX 7500 has a single XEON L5410 processor with 4 cores.

The MPX 10500 has dual QUAD Core XEON E5440 processors.

Since they all share the same X7DCU motherboard you can upgrade the CPU's in the lower model numbers (5500 & 7500) to match the CPU configuration of the 10500 (dual QUAD E5440). Keep in mind that you may need to upgrade the 300W power supply of the MPX 5500, depending on what you wish to accomplish. Luckily, the MPX 7500 shares the same dual, hot swappable 450W power supplies as the 10500, so upgrading the CPUs on this model will be no problem.

The down side of the X7-DCU based systems is limited internal power cables to power additional devices like hard drives and the lack of VT-d (I/O virtualization).

X9SPU MOTHERBOARD - MPX 8200

The Supermicro X9-SPU motherboard powers the MPX/SDX 8200

The MPX/SDX 8200 is not EOL until 2024, but it is often available used on eBay. As mentioned before; it runs a very powerful 3.4GHz 4-Core XEON E1275 v2 processor with hyper-threading yielding 8-threads, and comes with 32GB RAM. It runs very quiet (almost no fan noise). It can make a very good 1U project server if you get it cheap enough.

Supermicro says all there X9 series motherboards support SR-IOV.

```
Aptio Setup Utility - Copyright (C) 2011 American Megatrends, Inc.
  Advanced

 Integrated IO Configuration                        Check to enable VT-d
                                                     function on MCH.
 IIO Revision                    D2

 Intel VT-d                      [Enabled]
 Active State Power Management   [Auto]
 PCIe Maximum Read Request       [Auto]

 PCI Express Port                [Auto]

 PCI Express Port - Gen X        [Auto]
 De-emphasis Control             [-3.5 dB]

 Aperture Size                   [256MB]          ↔: Select Screen
 DVMT Pre-Allocated              [64M]            ↑↓: Select Item
 DVMT Total Gfx Mem              [256M]           Enter: Select
 Gfx Low Power Mode              [Enabled]        +/-: Change Opt.
 Graphics Performance Analyzers  [Disabled]       F1: General Help
▶ GT - Power Management Control                   F2: Previous Values
                                                  F3: Optimized Defaults
                                                  F4: Save & Exit
                                                  ESC: Exit


         Version 2.14.1219. Copyright (C) 2011 American Megatrends, Inc.
```

Make sure you have VT-d 'Enabled' and Active State Power Management

(ASPM) set to 'Auto'. You will need these settings in order to do PCIe passthrough for the Crypto cards, details in *Chapter 5 "NetScaler SDX - IDC in a BOX"*

X8DTE-F MOTHERBOARD - MPX 11500

NetScaler MPX 11500 contains the Supermicro X8DTE-F motherboard

The MPX 11500 is based on the Supermicro X8DTE-F motherboard and has dual HEX (6) Core XEON E5645 processors, running at 2.4GHz. That's 12 cores and 24 threads with hyper threading.

The MPX 11500 supports not only VT (virtualization) but also VT-d (I/O virtualization) also know as PCIe passthrough.

It you have the MPX/SDX 11500 you have a very power server platform and you can do just about anything you want with it.

Depending on your needs and because of its power, it may be best to use it as a virtualization platform rather then a dedicated server. We will discuss "NetScaler as a Virtualization Platform" in the next chapter, Chapter 4.

NETSCALER AS VIRTUALIZATION PLATFORM

Can Legacy NetScaler Run VMware ESXi Or Citrix XenServer?

VMware ESXi 6.5 fully supported (MPX 5500 and newer)

Citrix XenServer 7 fully supported (MPX 5500 and newer)

All Network Cards fully supported

Booting from Compact Flash (CF) fully supported (when included)

Exception - NetScaler MPX 11500 and MPX 8200 supports ESXi 6.7

Perhaps not "officially" supported in the VMware Hardware Compatibility List (HCL), these legacy NetScaler devices all support running both VMware ESXi 6.5+ and Citrix XenServer 7.0 hypervisors.

Best practice would be to use external SAN / NAS / iSCSI storage (covered in Chapter 6) but local (on board) storage can also be used for this application as well. Remember to enable SATA ports in BIOS before attempting to connect internal SATA drives to your NetScaler.

Regardless of which hypervisor you decide to deploy, you will discover that these legacy NetScalers can preform quite well as virtualization platforms.

One thing to remember is the 5500/7500/10500 CPU's do not support VT-d. This means you can not do PCIe re-direction on these systems like you can on the newer MPX 8200 and MPX 11500 platforms.

VT-d will be discussed in more detail in the next chapter, *Chapter 5*

"IDC In A Box".

NETSCALER SDX - IDC IN A BOX

My flyer for "IDC IN A BOX"

Using Newer MPX/SDX 8000/11500 Series

With VT-d supported CPUs you can do more with these newer platforms

End-to-End Hardware accelerated encryption is possible

Ability to use the built in Crypto-Cards

Do things Citrix states are "impossible"

What Is IDC In A Box?

The idea behind "IDC IN A BOX" is to have a single 1U or 2U device capable of doing hardware accelerated end-to-end encryption, contains its own internal storage as well as host a full stack of applications. My solution requires a Citrix NetScaler ADC with Crypto boards running VMware ESXi 6.5 or higher.

One deployment example would be a HA pair of NetScaler VPX's plus a complete Xen App/Xen Desktop deployment on a single server. Another example would be a HA pair of NetScaler VPX's plus a complete Internet Hosting Solution providing users with Web Hosting, E-mail and remote access to their sites.

Until now, we have been mostly discussing the first generation of MPX hardware, the MPX 5500/7500/10500 platforms. Everything you can do with this first generation of MPX appliances you can do with 2nd generation MPX appliances.

Specifically, for this "IDC In A Box" idea, I like to bring your attention to the 2nd generation; the MPX/SDX 8200/11500 series hardware.

While the MPX 8200 and MPX 11500 do not share the same motherboard they do share something very important, namely native support for Intel VT-d.

VT-d allows for I/O virtualization.

With VT-d you can assign PCIe and other hardware components directly to individual virtual machines. This means, for example, you can assign SATA ports to a VM running FreeNAS or assign Crypto-Chips to any virtual machine (VM) that recognizes SSL/TLS hardware acceleration.

* FYI: In 2020, I sold and signed-away my patent rights for my invention known as "IDC In A Box" to IBM. I retain all right to the product name "IDC In A Box". For now, IBM has decided to publish the details, rather then go for a patent. *

HARDWARE ACCELERATED CRYPTOGRAPHY

CRYPTO BOARDS FROM CAVIUM

Citrix claims there is no Cryptographic hardware acceleration possible for Citrix NetScaler VPX. VPX is the Citrix NetScaler virtual appliance that can run on various hypervisors. This never made sense to me since the Citrix NetScaler SDX is a custom "XenServer hypervisor" running multiple copies of VPX on a Citrix box which **DOES** provide Cryptographic hardware acceleration.

Until Intel provided Cryptographic hardware acceleration directly in their CPUs, Citrix has used Cavium (now owned by Marvell) Crypto boards to offload the SSL/TLS key generation. Hardware acceleration allows for faster SSL/TLS connection times as well as higher connection density (more simultaneous users). This is what is know as SSL/TLS hardware acceleration.

Can we utilize this hardware acceleration outside of NetScaler SDX? The short answer is YES!

First, you need a server with a VT-d capable CPU. The MPX/SDX 8200 & 11500 and newer meet these requirements.

Next we'll look at configuring PCI passthrough for the Crypo-cores.

CONFIG PCI PASSTHROUGH FOR CRYPTO

SINGLE HOST CONFIG

If you are running a single VMware ESXi host you can configure 'passthrough' directly on the host. After logging into the ESXi host UI (usually https://<host name or IP>/ui/) you'll navigate to **Host -> Manage -> Hardware -> PCI Devices -> Configure Passthrough**

and then configure your PCI Passthrough. Select any or all of the **"Nitrox XL NPX"** devices and then select TOGGLE PASSTHROUGH (on the top left).

A reboot of the host will be required before this PCI passthrough will become effective.

MULTI HOST CONFIGURATION

If you are running a multi ESXi host environment, you'll most likely be also running the **VMware vCenter Server Appliance (VCSA)**. If this is the case, you should log into the vSphere Client to do your PCI passthrough configuration.

Now select the HOST you will configure.

Click on **CONFIGURE -> Hardware -> PCI Devices -> Configure Passthrough**

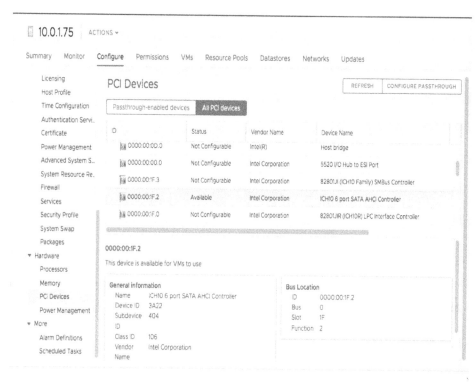

Here you can select the PCI component you wish to configure, in this case the **"Nitrox XL NPX"** (not shown in the photo above).

Reboot the host for the PCI passthrough to become active.

ADDING CRYPTO CORES TO YOUR VM

After reboot, the Crypto cores that you configured for passthrough will be available to assign to virtual machines. Now lets assign some crypto cores to your Virtual machines, in this case your NetScaler VPX running on VMware ESXi!

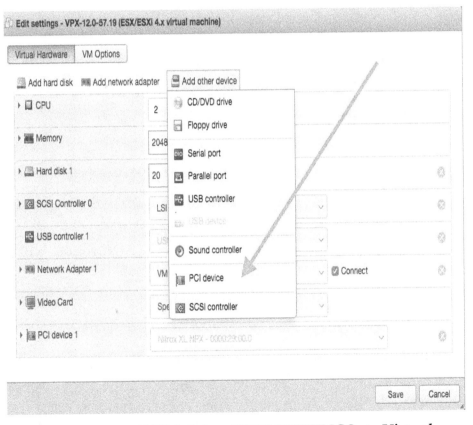

Select your VPX VM. Select **EDIT SETTINGS -> Virtual Hardware -> Add Other Device -> PCI Device**

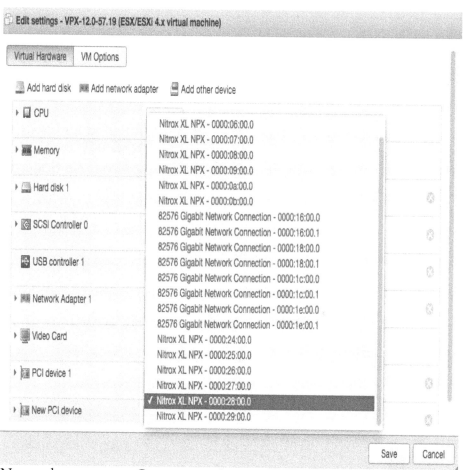

Now select your -> Crypto core instance (i.e. Nitrox XL NPX)

*Be sure each Crypto assignment is unique;
do not assign the same Crypto core more than once*

After assigning the Crypto core(s) you will also have to also assign memory to the Reservation part of your VM settings. The VM will not start with out this change. Go to **Edit Settings -> Virtual Hardware -> Memory**

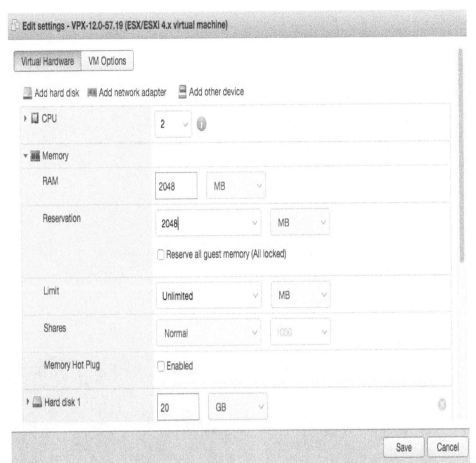

Assign the same amount of memory to Reservation as is assigned to the VPX. In this case we assign 2048 MB to the memory Reservation as 2048 MB is assigned to the VM itself.

Now you can boot up the VPX VM and crypto core(s) will be assigned to this virtual machine. In this example, I only assigned 1 crypto core to this VPX virtual machine. 2 crypto cores is recommended.

Hardware Configuration	
▸ 🖥 CPU	2 vCPUs
🖥 Memory	2 GB
▸ 💾 Hard disk 1	20 GB
🔌 USB controller	USB 2.0
▸ 🖧 Network adapter 1	VM Network (Connected)
▸ 🖥 Video card	4 MB
🖬 PCI device 1	Nitrox XL NPX
▸ 🖬 Others	Additional Hardware

From the NetScaler CLI you can check **"show ssl stats"** to see your hardware crypto is available:

```
SSL Summary

# SSL cards present            1
# SSL cards UP                 1
SSL engine status              0
SSL sessions (Rate)            0
```

From the NetScaler VPX GUI under Dashboard (SSL) you can see the same:

SSL ▾ ⌁ Graphic... ▤ Summary ✿ Default Group ↻ Refresh ⊠ Clear Help ⊟

# SSL cards present	1
# SSL cards UP	1
SSL engine status	0

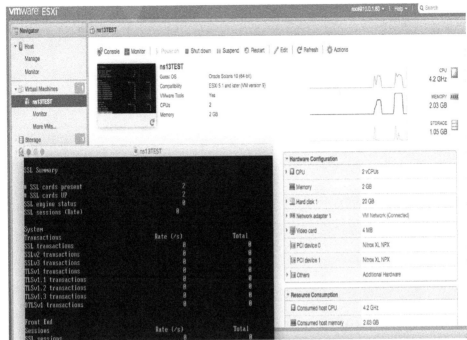

Here is another example with 2 Crypto Cards assigned to the VPX

Now, when you configure any SSL vServer on this NetScaler VPX, the crypto hardware will be utilized and this usage will be updated in the SSL STATS.

Check it out!

IDC IN A BOX NEXT STEPS

Licenses

Manage Licenses...

License type	Standard		Model ID	20
Load Balancing	✓		SSL Offloading	✓
Content Switching	✓		Cache Redirection	✓
Global Server Load Balancing	✗		GSLB Proximity	✗
Authentication, Authorization and Auditing	✗		NetScaler Gateway	✗
Maximum NetScaler Gateway Users Allowed	✗		Maximum ICA Users Allowed	✗
Clustering	✗		Web Interface	✓
Integrated Caching	✗		Front End Optimization	✗
Rewrite	✓		Responder	✓
HTTP Compression	✗		Content Filtering	✓
Application Firewall	✗		Cloud Bridge	✗
Priority Queuing	✗		Sure Connect	✗
Surge Protection	✗		DoS Protection	✗
AppFlow	✓		AppFlow for ICA	✗
IPv6 Protocol Translation	✓		Dynamic Routing	✗
BGP Routing	✗		OSPF Routing	✗
RIP Routing	✗		ISIS Routing	✗
Content Accelerator	✗		AppQoE	✗
NetScaler Push	✗	Free Version	Web Logging	✓
vPath	✗		RISE	✗
Callhome	✓		Large Scale NAT	✗
RDP Proxy	✗		Licensing Mode	EXPRESS
Reputation	✗		Delta Compression	✗
URL Filtering	✗		SSL Interception	✗
Forward Proxy	✗		Video Optimization	✗
Adaptive TCP	✗		Connection Quality Analytics	✗
Remote Content Inspection	✗			

Keep in mind that the Express/Standard (whatever Citrix is calling the free version these days) VPX license allows for SSL ofloading. So "IDC

In A Box" will work with the "Free" Express version of VPX, available from www.Citrix.com

Once you have hardware accelerated crypto on your VMware ESXi server working, you can install the remaining components of your Application Stack. Your Application Stack can be what ever can be run comfortably on your 1U or 2U server.

In my lab, I have gotten an entire XA/XD/PVS environment with VPX running on a single stock NetScaler 11500.

Perhaps, you will install a 2nd NetScaler VPX, assign it crypto cores and place your 2 VPX's in a HA pair.

If any component of the application stack knows how to use hardware acceleration, i.e. has drivers for this (many Linux distributions do) you can assign crypto cores to these virtual machines as well.

If configured correctly, any SSL/TLS traffic to and from this NetScaler "IDC In A Box" will have hardware accelerated SSL/TLS Cryptography. Since all internal traffic - between the NetScaler VPX and your Application Stack happens inside your ESXi server - you will have end-to-end encryption from this single server.

LINKS:

www.citrix.com

## Chapter 6

NETSCALER AS NAS/SAN STORAGE

The Legacy NetScaler MPX Can Run FreeNAS

Dedicated FreeNAS on legacy MPX hardware

Boot off CF supported

iSCSI/CIFS/AFS/NFS and more all supported

Consider running FreeNAS as a dedicated server load on legacy 1st generation NetScaler MPX hardware. You can have up to 6-internal SATA II drives, 48 GB RAM, and Dual Quad Core XEONS. That is more than enough power to provide iSCSI/CIFS and other file shares with advanced features like compression and de-duplication enabled.

In addition, such a system can run PLEX in a FreeNAS jail providing you easy access to all your media (movies, pictures, home videos).

FreeNAS requires a separate disk to boot from. It is recommended you use a 8GB USB memory stick or CF card to boot from. There is an internal USB port on the X7DCU motherboard that can work perfectly for deploying the FreeNAS application. Or if your NetScaler has a CF reader, you could use that.

LINKS:

https://www.freenas.org

VIRTUAL NAS / FREENAS

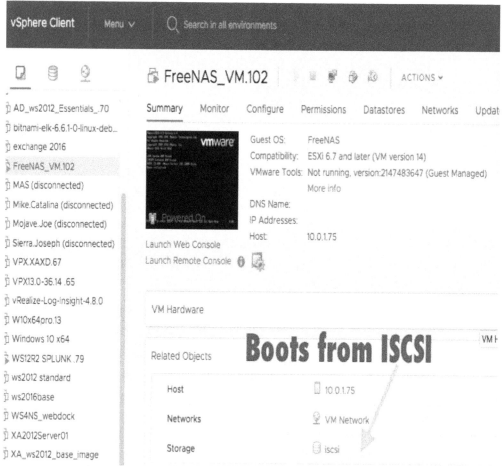

Virtual FreeNAS booting from shared iSCSI storage

Do you run VMware vSAN? That requires at least 3 servers and a vSAN license!

Do you connect to a separate iSCSI storage server? This requires additional configurations and connectivity to a separate storage server.

Would it be nice if you could have compute power and storage in a single box? Well "Virtual FreeNAS" could be your solution!

While not considered "best practice", it is possible to run FreeNAS as a virtual machine. To do this you will need to assign your SATA ports to the FreeNAS virtual machine using PCIe passthrough. This is possible with machines that have CPU's with VT-d capability, namely the MPX/SDX 8200 , 11500 and newer.

This process assumes you are booting ESXi from a USB Stick and not using any internal drive to boot ESXi

Create a FreeNAS virtual Machine

First, start the configuration of a new FreeNAS Virtual Machine as you would any normal virtual machine. But do NOT *Start Up* the new FreeNAS machine yet!

Let's now configure the SATA controller to be "owned" by this new FreeNAS virtual machine.

SINGLE HOST CONFIG

If you are running a single VMware ESXi host you can configure SATA passthrough directly on the host. After logging into the ESXi host UI (usually https://<host name or IP>/ui/) you'll navigate to **Host -> Manage -> Hardware** and then configure your SATA Passthrough. A reboot of the host will be required before this SATA passthrough will become effective.

MULTI HOST CONFIGURATION

If you are running a multi ESXi host environment, you'll most likely be also running the **VMware vCenter Server Appliance (VCSA)**. If this is the case, you should log into the vSphere Client to do this SATA passthrough configuration.

Now select the HOST you will configure.

Click on **CONFIGURE -> Hardware -> PCI Devices**

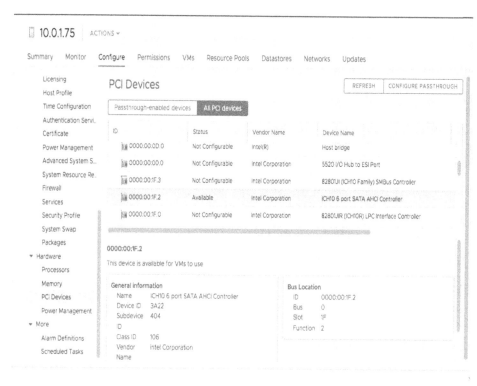

Here you can select the PCI component you wish to configure, in this case the **"ICHI0 6 port SATA AHCI Controller"** (on the MPX 11500)

Reboot the host for the PCI passthrough to become active.

Edit Setting of your FreeNAS virtual Machine

After re-boot, the SATA ports are available to assign to a virtual Machine. Log back into your **https://<host name>/ui**

Select your FreeNAS virtual machine and click EDIT SETTINGS.

Click ADD NEW DEVICE and select the **"ICHI0 6 port SATA AHCI Controller"**. Click OK

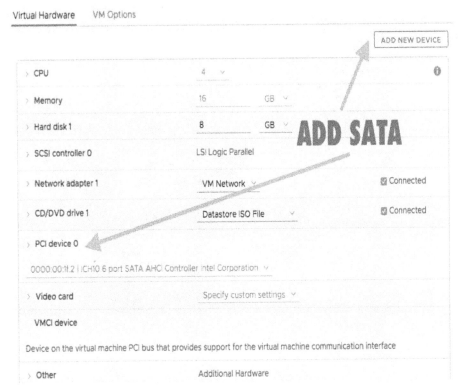

Now you can start up your FreeNAS VM and configure as usual. What ever SSD or mechanical hard drives you have attached to your SATA ports will now be available for FreeNAS to add to any pools you wish to create.

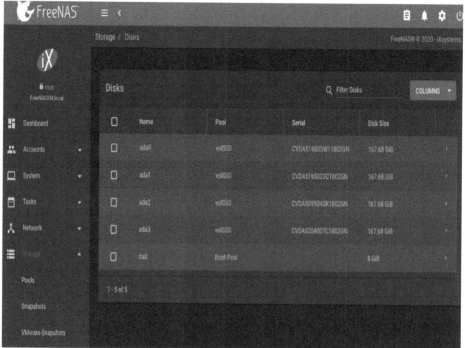

Disks shown as available in FreeNAS 11.3

Considerations

When using virtual FreeNAS, keep in mind that this FreeNAS virtual machine must be up and running first. That is, before anything (VM, CIFS storage, etc.) that is dependent upon this storage can be accessed.

The reverse is also true when it comes to shutting down the FreeNAS VM. You must be sure that anything (VM, CIFS storage, etc.) that might be accessing the FreeNAS storage is shutdown before shutting down the FreeNAS VM.

In my case, I need to make sure my iSCSI shared storage is up and running before I power on the ESXi host that runs my FreeNAS VM. That is because the FreeNAS VM itself is stored on my 'remote' iSCSI storage. In addition, I have enabled AUTOSTART for this FreeNAS VM, so that as soon as the ESXi Host powers up, the FreeNAS VM is immediately started.

HOST->Config ->Virtual Machines ->VM Startup/Shutdown

Also, keep in mind that because this FreeNAS VM is dependent on drives physically in this particular ESXi host, I can not "migrate" or 'vMotion" this FreeNAS VM to another host.

For my lab environment and for testing, this is an acceptable solution. My performance is actually quite good, due to the ZFS 'raid' configuration I have as well as 4 SSD's available in the pool.

The alternative and "best practice" to this virtualized approach is to deploy FreeNAS on dedicated NetScaler hardware. This is discussed in *"Chapter 3: NetScaler as a Dedicated Server."*

## Chapter 7

NETSCALER AS A 10GB SWITCH

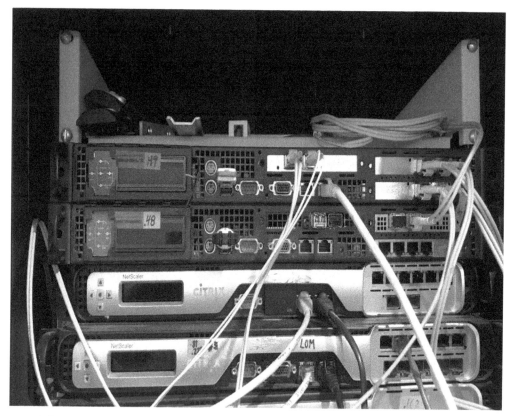

The Legacy MPX Platform Can Be Converted Into A 10Gb Switch

VyOS open source network switch software fully supported

The MPX 5500 & 7500 offer the best value

Up to 3 Dual 10Gb cards can be added to the MPX 5500 & 7500 platforms

The MPX 10500 is not recommended as it does not contain enough x8 PCI slots

Very low cost way to build your own 10Gb/s switch

The 1U riser card in the MPX 5500 / 7500 contains three (3) x8 PCIe slots. This means you can replace the existing network and crypto boards with Dual 10Gb network cards.

In my experience, 7+ Gb/s speeds were achieved using this hardware. While it is short of the 10 Gb/s speed the network cards are capable of, it is more then 7x faster then the 1 Gb/s network cards you may be currently using.

VYOS ON NETSCALER HARDWARE

```
File  Edit  View  Terminal  Tabs  Help
vyos@vyos-test-2# set protocols static route 192.0.2.0/24 blackhole
[edit]
vyos@vyos-test-2# show protocols static
+route 192.0.2.0/24 {
+    blackhole {
+    }
+}
[edit]
vyos@vyos-test-2# commit
[edit]
vyos@vyos-test-2# show protocols static route
 route 192.0.2.0/24 {
     blackhole {
     }
 }
[edit]
vyos@vyos-test-2# run show ip route
Codes: K - kernel route, C - connected, S - static, R - RIP, O - OSPF,
       I - ISIS, B - BGP, > - selected route, * - FIB route

S>* 0.0.0.0/0 [210/0] via 10.46.1.254, eth0
C>* 10.46.1.0/24 is directly connected, eth0
C>* 10.94.0.0/24 is directly connected, dum0
C>* 127.0.0.0/8 is directly connected, lo
S>* 192.0.2.0/24 [1/0] is directly connected, Null0, bh
[edit]
vyos@vyos-test-2#
```

I have converted 2 NetScalers into 10Gb VyOS switches.

VyOS is open source Network Switch software which can be run as a Virtual Machine or directly on bare metal hardware.

My first project was done using a NetScaler MPX 7500. I removed the crypto boards and made space for (2) two DUAL PORT 10Gb Network cards from Chelsio (model 110). You will have to do additional research, but many other 10Gb cards are supported.

The second was a MPX 5500. Again I removed the crypto boards and the network card. This time I added (3) three DUAL PORT 10Gb Network cards from Chelsio.

What You Need

You will need to have 2 USB memory sticks for this project. One for the bootable .ISO installer (reusable) and the other for the destination, which will run VyOS on your NetScaler permanently.

One memory "stick" could actually be a CF card, if you are using a NetScaler with a CF card reader! The destination memory stick (or CF) only needs be 2GB.

Download and install the "VyOS installer .ISO" file to your PC or Mac. Now use a tool like **RUFUS** to make one of your USB sticks a bootable image of this .ISO file.

Installation is really straight forward.

Insert both USB sticks (installer and destination) in the NetScaler

Boot from the Installer USB stick

Install VyOS to the second USB stick (or CF card), your destination USB drive

Reboot and remove the installer USB

Boot from the 2nd USB stick(or CF card)

Configure VyOS how you like

After logging in (the default username and password is "vyos"), you will be in the 'operation mode'.

Some **helpful operation commands** you might need:

show conf commands

show int eth eth3 identify (blinks the interface port eth3)

show ntp

ntpq -p   (will test the time server)

sudo ifconfig -s (verify MTU settings)

you can type **config** to enter the configuration mode, type **exit** to leave configuration mode.

Some <u>helpful configuration commands</u> you might need, TAB based auto complete does work in most cases:

set sys host-name <name>

set sys gateway-address <ip>

set sys name-server <ip>

set sys time-zone <Continent/City>

set int bridge br0 desc "10 Gb Switch"   (define your bridge 'br0' and give it a name)

set int eth eth1 bridge-group bridge br0 (add ethernet interface eth1 to the bridge) do this for all the ports you want to add to the bridge

set int bridge br0 address <ip/netmask> (set the management address for your bridge)

set service ssh listen -address <ip> (SSH traffic usually on your management IP)

set int eth eth7 mtu 9000   (set MTU on 10Gb port 'eth7' to 9000)

After making configuration changes, you issue the "**commit**" command to confirm the changes followed by "**save**" to save the changes to your configuration file.

There are many good configuration resources on the VyOS website as well as many example deployments on youTube.com.

This is an excellent way to extend the life of the MPX 5500/7500 hardware. While the MPX 10500 comes with 1 DUAL PORT 10Gb card and 8 x 1GB ports, and it could make a fantastic VyOS switch, but it makes little sense. The riser card in the 10500 only has one (1) PCIe x8 port and the 10Gb card is already using it. The remaining PCIe 4x port will not support a 10Gb interface card.

LINKS:

https://www.vyos.io

https://rufus.ie

## Chapter 8

CONVERTING THE BR-SDX TO SDX

```
FreeDOS kernel build 2036 cvs [version Aug 18 2006 compiled Aug 18 2006]
kernel compatibility 7.10 - WATCOMC - 80386 CPU required - FAT32 support

(C) Copyright 1995-2006 Pasquale J. Villani and The FreeDOS Project.
All Rights Reserved. This is free software and comes with ABSOLUTELY NO
WARRANTY; you can redistribute it and/or modify it under the terms of the
GNU General Public License as published by the Free Software Foundation;
either version 2, or (at your option) any later version.
 - InitDiskWARNING: Partition ID does not suggest LBA - part Pri:1 FS 0b.
Please run FDISK to correct this - using LBA to access partition.
 start     0-1-1, end 1304-254-63
C: HD1, Pri[ 1], CHS=    0-1-1, start=     0 MB, size= 10236 MB

FreeCom version 0.84-pre2 XMS_Swap [Aug 28 2006 00:29:00]
Checking the system...
Manufacturing for BRonSDX with 1400120
Error: No BRonSDX configuration for [1400120]
ERROR! ERROR! ERROR!
MPX to SDX conversion is not supported for this system
Please power off the system and remove this SSD drive
ERROR! ERROR! ERROR!
c:\boot\syslinux\sl_fdos.cfg => c:\boot\syslinux\syslinux.cfg
STAGE0 ready to run!
REBOOT SYSTEM!
C:\>
```

Hacking The "BR SDX Can Not Be Converted To SDX" Problem

The BR-SDX and SDX share the exact same hardware.

The MPX to SDX upgrade process fails (without hacks)

Did you purchase the "SDX Branch Repeater" or BR-SDX 11500,

thinking it was just a 'normal' MPX/SDX 11500. Thats what happened to me. Physically, it contains the same hardware, and basically is the same appliance with a few changes.

In this chapter, I will take you through the steps it takes to convert your BR-SDX to a normal SDX. If you have the SDX boot disk then you already have everything you need.

First, lets understand why your BR-SDX would not convert to a standard SDX.

Well, its because the serial number and model name that Citrix gave that appliance tells the installer it is a BR-SDX and not a normal MPX/SDX. As a result, it refuses to upgrade. So what you need is a new "MPX/SDX 11500" serial number. Where to get one? Well eBay of course! And the best thing is it's free. Just search for "NetScaler MPX 11500" on sale on eBay and look for sellers who expose their "System Information" screen. Or ask the seller to show you the "system information" screen so you can confirm your interest.

Download the image to your computer and zoom in on the serial number!

Platform	NSMPX-11500 12*CPU+2*E1K+8*E1K+4*IX+16*CVM 1620 14001
Manufactured on	1/14/2013
CPU	2400 MHZ
Host Id	872841350
Serial no	JH2PD27SE3
Encoded serial no	JH2PD27SE3
Netscaler UUID	d1567a0e-a5d2-11e8-ba10-00e0ed22298a

This one looks like JH2PD27SE3.

Serial Numbers are all-caps-alpha and numbers only.

Citrix NetScaler SDX 14000 No Hard Drives in bays at back, sold without licenses Serial Number: M8G5MCVTPV Label on case says: 2U1P1B Screen on startup states: Citrix NSSDX-14000

Another example of info gathered from the web/eBay

DMICFG TO UPDATE DMI/SMBIOS INFORMATION

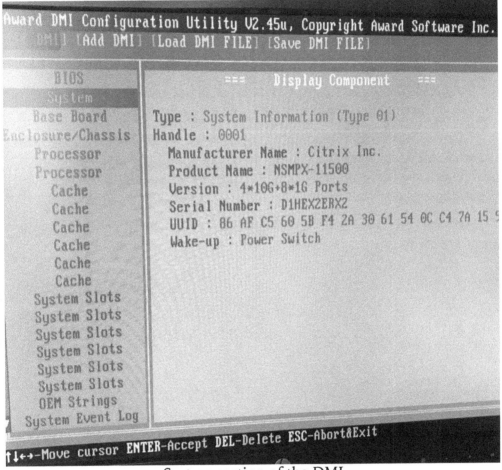

System section of the DMI

DMICFG.EXE for DOS

(ftp://ftp.supermicro.com/utility/DMI/AWARD/DMICFG.EXE) may be
used to update the Serial Number and some other fields in the

DMI/SMBIOS table.

The DMICFG.exe utility is also on the primary boot partition of your SDX Boot disk, which is a FreeDOS partition. File location on boot disk is: **C:/TOOLS/DMICFG**

The easiest way to run this utility is to create a FreeDOS boot USB using the **RUFUS** utility. Then copy the DMICFG.EXE executable to this USB stick.

Next, insert the FreeDOS USB stick into your BR-SDX and boot from this USB stick. Next, execute the DMICFG.exe and make the required changes to the "**System**" section of the DMI.

You will need to change the Product Name and the Serial Number to match the new Serial Number you have acquired.

Once this is accomplished, you can reboot the NetScaler and boot from the MPX to SDX conversion "boot" disk and this device will be recognized as either an MPX or SDX and the upgrade process will proceed normally.

Please only do this on a real BR-SDX. I would not try this on any other hardware.

LINKS:

ftp://ftp.supermicro.com/utility/DMI/AWARD/DMICFG.EXE

https://rufus.ie

## Chapter 9

NETSCALER HACKENTOSH

Your Legacy MPX 5500/7500/10500 Can Run Mac OS As A Hackentosh

Yosemite OS X 10.10

El Capitan OS X 10.11

Sierra OS X 10.12

High Sierra OS X 10.13

Mojave OS X 10.14 (requires SSE 4.1 patch on older CPUs)

Catalina OS X 10.15 (requires SSE 4.1 patch on older CPUs)

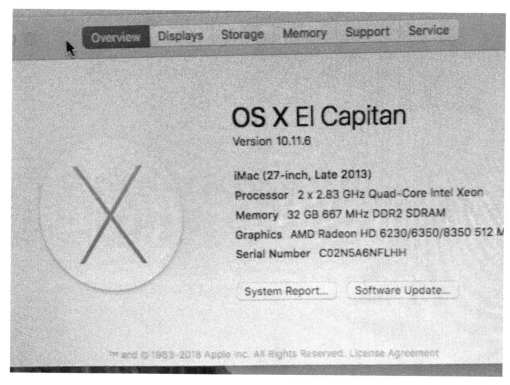

Dual Quad Core MPX 10500 running ElCapitan

PRO-TIP: Be sure to remove any CryptoBoards from your NetScaler before starting

Cavium (now owned by Marvell) has been the supplier of Cryptographic-acceleration boards for the Citrix NetScaler. They are not needed by MacOS and should be removed. But don't throw them away, as detailed in Chapter 5 "IDC In A Box" they can still be used for other deployments / applications.

Using the tools provided by TonyMacX86.com you can run OS X on the legacy Citrix NetScaler MPX hardware. I have had success installing Yosemite, El Capitan, Sierra and High Sierra on the NetScaler MPX 5500/7500/10500. These NetScaler models use the Supermicro X7-DCU motherboard and run on older CPUs with SSE 4.1 support.

Mojave and Catalina require SSE 4.2 support, so they can not run on these platforms with out modifications. There appears to be a "patch" that you can install to allow these 2 operating systems to run on your older CPUs. More on this later.

You will need the OS X version you want to install (Apple App Store), UniBeast and MultiBeast (from TonyMacX86.com).

There are many resources for turning your legacy hardware into a Hackentosh, many believe the best site is https://www.tonymacx86.com

OTHER LINKS:

https://www.tonymacx86.com

https://www.insanelymac.com

https://www.dosdude1.com (only works on real Apple Hardware)

MAJOR STEPS FOR NETSCALER HACKENTOSH

Get the actual procedure from the appropriate https://www.tonymacx86.com installation guides. It will require a free account to get access to all the files you need.

Download the OS X version that you want to install.

Then run UniBeast to create the bootable USB for that OS X

Install OS X on the NetScaler to an internal disk.

Now post install, run MultiBeast to configure the Hackentosh to boot from the hard drive and add needed features (network, SATA, model number)

Optional: Install any graphics card and drivers (outside the scope of this book, but discussed in "Section 5: Graphic Cards for Hackentosh")

Even with the low quality graphics card that comes on the motherboard (ATI Radon HD 4330M), you can still make use of this Hackentosh as a generic computer, a OS X file server or "OS X Server". You will not be able to run graphic-intensive programs like FCPX until you upgrade to a more powerful GPU.

If you do upgrade the GPU and install the required drivers (or patches or kext), be sure to disable the internal graphics in BIOS once you are sure the new graphics are working.

BIOS -> PCI CONFIGURATION -> Default Primary Video Adaptor.

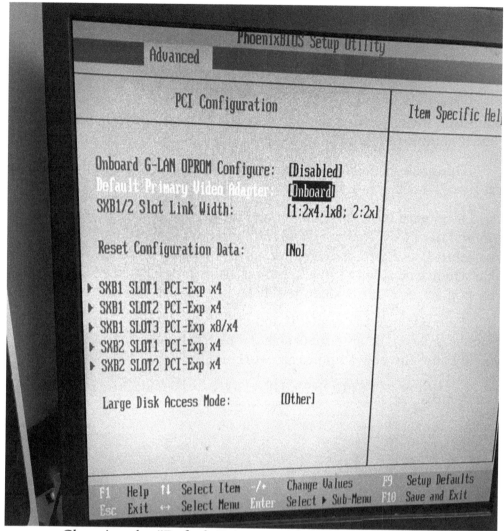

Inside the image:

PhoenixBIOS Setup Utility

Advanced

PCI Configuration

Item Specific Hel|

Onboard G-LAN OPROM Configure: [Disabled]
Default Primary Video Adapter: [Onboard]
SXB1/2 Slot Link Width: [1:2x4,1x8; 2:2x]

Reset Configuration Data: [No]

▶ SXB1 SLOT1 PCI-Exp x4
▶ SXB1 SLOT2 PCI-Exp x4
▶ SXB1 SLOT3 PCI-Exp x8/x4
▶ SXB2 SLOT1 PCI-Exp x4
▶ SXB2 SLOT2 PCI-Exp x4

Large Disk Access Mode: [Other]

F1 Help ↑↓ Select Item -/+ Change Values F9 Setup Defaults
Esc Exit ↔ Select Menu Enter Select ▶ Sub-Menu F10 Save and Exit

Changing the "Default Primary Video Adaptor" in BIOS

If you should run into any problems with this new video adaptor configuration, you can always go back into the BIOS and reset the "Default Primary Video Adaptor" back to "Onboard" and troubleshoot further.

INTERNAL SATA DRIVE CONFIGURATION

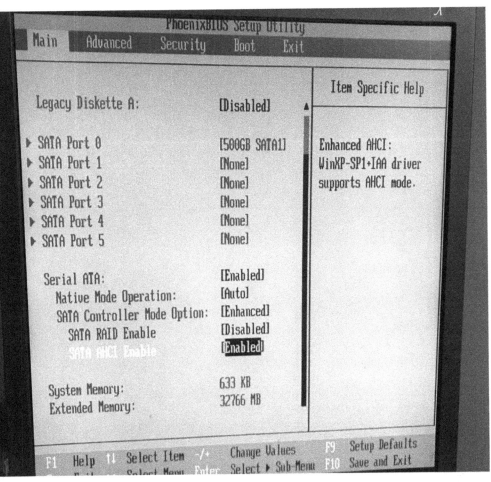

By default your NetScaler has its internal drive bays disabled. If your internal hard drive is not discovered by the Mac OS X installer you will have to enable SATA AHCI in BIOS.

On the X7-DCU based NetScalers (MPX 5500/7500/10500) you will need to change the default BIOS setting:

MAIN -> Serial ATA (SATA) -> SATA AHCI Enabled

Make sure you enable your SATA ports before you attempt to connect any internal drives on your "Netscaler Hackentosh".

PATCH SSE 4.1 CPU TO RUN MOJAVE & CATALINA?

DosDude1 (https://www.DOSDUDE1.com) released software to allow the **Apple xServe 2,1** running a similar CPU as the NetScaler MPX 10500 to run Mojave and Catalina. Based on this, I know there has to be a way to run SSE 4.2 required OS X versions on older CPUs with just SSE 4.1 hardware.

From my research, this solution is also how DOSDUDE1 has enabled Mojave and Catalina to run on even C2D (Core2Duo) based Apple hardware, like the 2009 iMac.

At the time of writing, I have not been able to get Mojave or Catalina to run on 5500/7500/10500 MPX hardware. I get the "unsupported CPU" error.

However, there appears to be a "patching" procedure to overcome SSE 4.1 limitations. The same details were posted on www.tonymacx86.com and www.insanelymac.com. It appears all you need to do is replace one file.

"There is no need to add and replace all the UserEventPlugins folder instead follow these steps:

leave the Mojave's System/Library/UserEventPlugins untouched;
- replace from a High Sierra's System/Library/UserEventPlugins just this plugin: com.apple.telemetry.plugin"

So according to these sources, you need to replace one file, the System/Library/UserEventPlugins/com.apple.telemetry.plugin file with the file of the same name from OS X version High Sierra or older.

I tried this re-place one file approach and it did not work for me. There may be something else missing. I will try this again and if I am successful I will post details on my website www.n90x.info.

Thus far, High Sierra is the highest version of OS X that I got running on MPX 5500/7500/10500 hardware.

If you find a way to get Mojave and Catalina to run on this older hardware before I do, please let me know.

MPX/SDX 11500 HACKENTOSH

Front metal frame removed

The MPX/SDX 11500 supports all current versions of OS X. The trick to get OS X installed is to remove all the Crypto and network cards.

First you need to remove the top cover from your MPX/SDX 11500. There are 3 screws on each side (one hidden under the white "CITRIX" sticker). One screw on the top center and one screw in the back center of the cover. Once all these screw are removed you can slide the cover to the rear. It will slide back about 1 inch and then you can lift the lid off.

With the top cover off, you can now remove the "plastic Citrix branded face plate". There is one screw on the right side of the front of the 11500 as you face it. Once this is remove you can gently pry the front cover off and remove the remaining screws that hold it. These screws need to be removed from inside the NetScaler.

Once the plastic Citrix face plate is remove we can advance to the front metal frame. There are 6 screws on the front metal panel that secure it to the server body. All the PCIe cards attach to this front metal frame as well. Remove all of these 6 screws as well as all of the screws that hold the PCIe cards to the front metal frame. Now you can remove this frame and the PCIe cards. As always, only connect or remove PCIe cards when the system is powered off and the power cable is disconnected.

During OS X installation, you'll need to disable VT-d and Virtualization in BIOS. Be sure to enable your SATA ports and select AHCI mode. You may have to switch to Single -Core for install.

I followed the Tonymacx86.com installation guide and booted Yosemite with the "boot -v -nv_disable" flags from a iBoot/Unibeast USB stick.

I did plug in a OS X compatible BlueTooth dongle, but I confirmed later, this is not necessary to boot from USB and install OS X Yosemite.

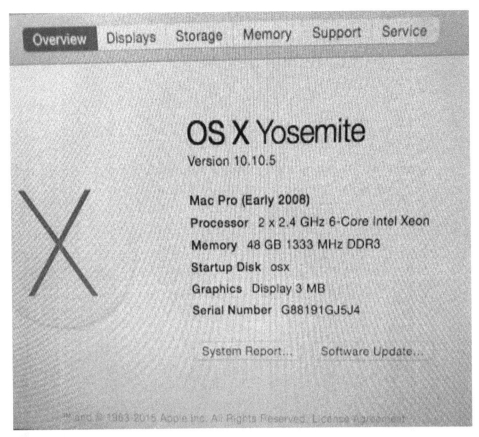

After Yosemite installed, I ran MultiBeast to install the various kext needed and to make the hard disk bootable. I restarted the machine and removed the USB stick. When the system tried to boot from the hard drive for the first time I got the following series of errors on a black screen:

boot0: GPT

boot0: test

boot0: test

boot0: test

boot0: GPT

boot0: test

boot0: test

boot0: test

boot0: error_

If you get this error

To resolve this situation, you need to re-insert your bootable USB stick, reboot and boot off the USB stick. This will start the installer, but we do NOT want to reinstall YOSEMITE.

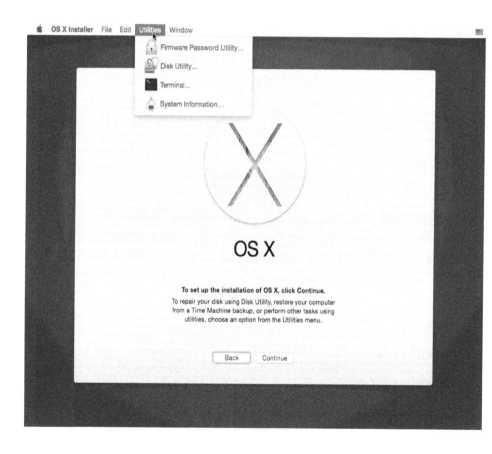

Go to the top menu bar, select UTILITIES -> Disk UTILITY and select your hard drive. Press "Command + i " ("windows key + i " if you are using a PC keyboard) to get information on your drive. Note the disk name, also known as the **Disk Identifier**. You want to know the drive name, i.e. **disk0s2**

Now if you right click on your drive name, you can **UNMOUNT** your hard drive and close Disk Utility.

Next, open the Utilities -> Terminal and type in the follow line:

dd if=/usr/standalone/i386/boot1h of=/dev/disk0s2

(remember to replace disk0s2 with your disk identifier if it is different then mine)

You should get a message on the terminal about "Records in" and "Records out" and how many bytes were transferred. If you get this you are good and can reboot the machine, pull out the boot USB stick and boot directly off the hard drive!

Installing Newer Versions of OS X

Newer versions of OS X are to be installed in a similar manner. As I have time to install newer versions of OS X directly on the 11500 hardware I will provide updates on my website www.n90x.info , especially, if I discover something has changed in the procedure.

GRAPHIC CARDS FOR HACKENTOSH

GRAPHICS CARDS

Installing and configuring graphics cards is really beyond the scope of this book. That's because there are so many cards to choose from and often each card has a different procedure to use for each OS X flavor.

However, I do have several ATI Radeon HD 5450 cards (PCIe 1x versions) that I got cheaply on eBay. I plugged one into the MPX/SDX

11500 and connected up the DVI video output to a monitor. Of course only add or remove PCIe cards when the system is powered off and the power cable is disconnected!

I rebooted the system and without making any changes to the BIOS, the ATI Radeon HD 5450 took over the video output from the built-in graphics card. Wow! I now have 1080p Graphics now and while it's not perfect, its pretty fast and very usable.

====================================

BONUS Video POWER and USB Ports

Inside the MPX/SDX 11500

What's exciting about the MPX/SDX 11500 as Hackentosh is not only it's CPU power and memory capacity, but also its *electrical power*!

Unlike the MPX 10500 with limited internal power, once you remove the 11500's Crypto boards you now can use the 2 (two) six-pin power cables to power a ***very powerful*** graphics card!

As a bonus, 2 internal USB ports are exposed for use as well!

Chapter 10

VIRTUAL NETSCALER HACKENTOSH

Running Mac OS X On Legacy NetScaler Hardware

NetScaler MPX 5500/7500/10500 can run up to OS X 10.12 Sierra (ESXi 6.5)

NetScaler MPX/SDX 11500 can run everything including OS X 10.14 Mojave and OS X 10.15 Catalina (ESXi 6.7)

In the previous chapter, we discussed using the NetScaler to run OS X directly on the hardware as a "Hackentosh". In this chapter we will discuss your options with running OS X as a virtual machine on legacy NetScaler Hardware.

Due to the limitations of ESXi 6.5; which is the latest ESXi version you can run on the MPX 5500/7500/10500 hardware, you will be limited to running up to OS X 10.12 Sierra as a virtual machine on this hardware..

However, since ESXi 6.7 can be run on the newer MPX/SDX 8000/11500 hardware you can also run all past OS X versions as well as OS X 10.14 Mojave and OS X 10.15 Catalina as virtual machines. Both Mojave and Catalina require CPU settings that are not available in older processors.

<u>UNLOCK YOUR BOX</u>

To get "virtual Hackentosh" to work on your NetScaler hardware you must first run an UNLOCKER program. This would not be required if you are running on actual Apple hardware like the Apple xServe Server or a MacMini.

Google "UNLOCKER ESXi" adding your ESXi version number to

find this utility. For example Google "UNLOCKER ESXi 6.7" . The website **INSANELYMac** https://www.insanelymac.com/ is a good source for this utility , but requires a free registration to obtain access. Make sure you get your **<u>unlocker</u>** program from a reliable source.

After "unlocking" your ESXi hardware you will see new **OS X** Virtual Machine options are now exposed when creating a new Virtual Machine.

CREATING A BOOTABLE .ISO FROM .DMG

To install a OS X virtual machine on ESXi you will need an .ISO version of the installer.

Download your "Install macOS version_name" (i.e.: **Install macOS Sierra**") file from the Apple Store, it should be automatically placed in your **Application folder**.

Open you **Application** folder and right-click on the file name. Select "show contents", now open the folder named **SharedSupport** and copy the file named "**InstallESD.dmg**" to your desktop.

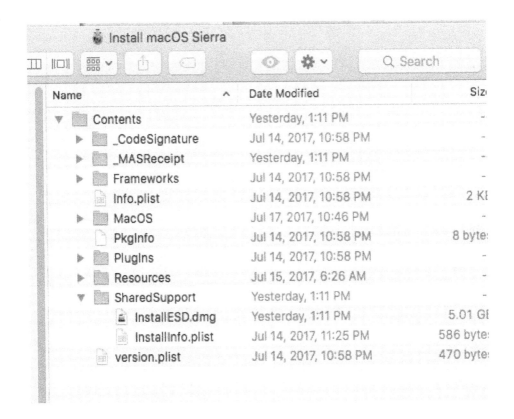

Open a terminal window and navigate to the Desktop and run this script (below) to create a bootable .ISO version of the .DMG installation media. This script is looking for "InstallESD.dmg" and will create "Maverick.iso". If you are converting a different version of OS X, feel free to search & replace all Maverick occurrences with the actual name of the OS X you wish to convert.

```
#!/bin/bash

# Verify that InstallESD.dmg exists

if [ ! -f ~/Desktop/InstallESD.dmg ]; then

    echo "InstallESD.dmg not found on desktop!"

    exit 1

fi

# Mount the installer image
```

```
hdiutil attach ~/Desktop/InstallESD.dmg -noverify -nobrowse -mountpoint
/Volumes/install_app
```

Create the Maverick Blank ISO Image of 7316mb with a Single Partition - Apple Partition Map

```
hdiutil create -o /tmp/Maverick.cdr -size 7316m -layout SPUD -fs HFS+J
```

Mount the Maverick Blank ISO Image

```
hdiutil attach /tmp/Maverick.cdr.dmg -noverify -nobrowse -mountpoint
/Volumes/install_build
```

Restore the Base System into the Maverick Blank ISO Image

```
asr restore -source /Volumes/install_app/BaseSystem.dmg -target /Volumes/install_build
-noprompt -noverify -erase
```

Remove Package link and replace with actual files

```
rm /Volumes/OS\ X\ Base\ System/System/Installation/Packages
```

```
cp -rp /Volumes/install_app/Packages /Volumes/OS\ X\ Base\
System/System/Installation/
```

Copy El Capitan installer dependencies

```
cp -rp /Volumes/install_app/BaseSystem.chunklist /Volumes/OS\ X\ Base\
System/BaseSystem.chunklist
```

```
cp -rp /Volumes/install_app/BaseSystem.dmg /Volumes/OS\ X\ Base\
System/BaseSystem.dmg
```

Unmount the installer image

```
hdiutil detach /Volumes/install_app
```

Unmount the Maverick ISO Image

```
hdiutil detach /Volumes/OS\ X\ Base\ System/
```

Convert the Maverick ISO Image to ISO/CD master (Optional)

```
hdiutil convert /tmp/Maverick.cdr.dmg -format UDTO -o /tmp/Maverick.iso
```

Rename the Maverick ISO Image and move it to the desktop

```
mv /tmp/Maverick.iso.cdr ~/Desktop/Maverick.iso
```

For your convenience, I will place a copy of this script on my website https://www.n90x.info

MOJAVE AND CATALINA

To install Mojave or Catalina (or any other OS X version) on ESXi 6.7 you will need a bootable .ISO image of the OS X operating system. You can create your own bootable .ISO from Apple's **InstallESD.dmg** version of the OS that you acquired from the App Store, as detailed in the previous section.

Another option is to download a pre-made .ISO directly. Make sure you download any .iso installers from a reliable source.

Both of these operating systems (Mojave and Catalina) require that you enable the following CPU settings before installing. When creating the OS X Virtual Machine, or when the VM is powered off, Select VM -> EDIT SETTINGS

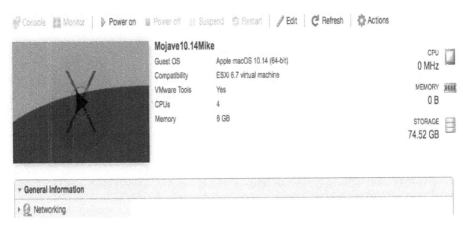

Click the down arrow by CPU and change the following CPU settings:

Hardware Virtualization: EXPOSE HARDWARE ASSISTED VIRTUALIZATION TO THE GUEST OS and

Performance Counters: ENABLE VIRTUALIZED CPU

PERFORMANCE COUNTERS

Once these settings are configured you can install and run your version of Mojave or Catalina.

XCODE DEVELOPER MACHINE - PRO-TIPS

One of the main reasons you might want to virtualize OS X is to use Xcode, Apples's IDE (Integrated Development Environment) used to develop iOS and Mac applications.

Xcode itself is free and can be downloaded from the OS X App Store, but it only runs on OS X. In addition, there are limitations on what version of Xcode can run on what version of OS X. If you want to run the latest version of Xcode, typically you will need the latest or just prior version of OS X.

For example, to run Xcode 11.0 you need Mojave OS X 14.4 or later.

If you have successfully installed OS X and Xcode you eventually will want to test your iOS application on real hardware. You may have noticed that if you connect your iPhone or iPad to your virtualized system it will continuously connect-and-disconnect. This prevents you from ever connecting your iPhone/iPad to Xcode.

Connect My iOS Device To Xcode

The solution is to insure you have a USB 2.0 controller assigned to your virtual machine (do this when powered off). If you find that a USB 3.0 controller is already assigned, delete it and then add a new USB 2.0 controller. With your iOS device connected to your physical server running the Virtual machine you should be able to also add "iPhone".

Now when you boot up your VM you may continue to see connection issues. If so, then power off the VM and download and open your "vmware.log" file. It will be located in the same folder where you installed your OS X virtual machine. Search for the following in your **vmware.log** file:

vmx | USB: Found device [name:Apple\ IR\ Receiver vid:05ac pid:12a8

Now download your VM's ".vmx" file to your PC/Mac and add the following line in an text editor:

usb.quirks.device0 = "0xvid:0xpid skip-reset, skip-refresh, skip-setconfig"

Replace 0xvid:0xpid by the vid & pid found in vmware.log. In my case, vid:05ac and pid:12a8 were found in my vmware.log file so I added the following line to my .vmx file:

usb.quirks.device0 = "0x05ac:0x12a8 skip-reset, skip-refresh, skip-setconfig"

** It makes sense to back up your current ".vmx" file before we do the next step.**

Now upload the modified ".vmx" file to the same location where you downloaded it. If you have not backed up (or renamed the old .vmx file) it will be over written.

Now when you power on the OS X virtual machine, the constant connect-reconnect will have stopped and your iOS device will be connected to your OS X virtual machine. Now you can go about connecting it up to Xcode for real hardware testing.

What About Audio For My OS X VM?

VMware clearly states "remote audio is not supported" in ESXi and if you need this feature, you should use their WORKSTATION or FUSION type-2 hypervisor products.

I've got good and bad news, first the bad news.

THE BAD NEWS

At first, the best I could accomplish was to add HD AUDIO to my OS X VM settings. Remember to do this when the VM is turned off. This will only produce "white noise" when your Xcode simulator (or any other player) produces audio. Not a perfect solution but at least you can run your app in the simulator and hear 'something'.

<u>USB Audio ?</u>

In my testing, I used an OS X compatible USB Audio device (C-Media). While you can connect this to your physical ESXi server and ADD this device to your OS X VM (Edit->Settings). You can even select this device from your Volume control dropdown (in OS X)! But still no audio will be produced, even though it looks like audio data is being sent to the USB device.

<u>Bluetooth Audio?</u>

I tested a known OS X compatible Bluetooth dongle (Broadcom BCM2045) and while I could add it to the OS X VM it never appeared in System Preferences -> Bluetooth.

<u>Jaber 370 Audio?</u>

I even tried my Jabber 370 dongle and headset, but again no luck.

THE GOOD NEWS (finally)

<u>Airport Express Speakers Audio</u>?

Under my OS X volume control this whole time was my "Airport Express Speakers." I had ignored it because it sits on the first floor and I work on the 2nd floor. But now it was my final hope. So I switched to "Airport Express Speakers" I started playing an .mp3 file and ran downstairs with my headphones.

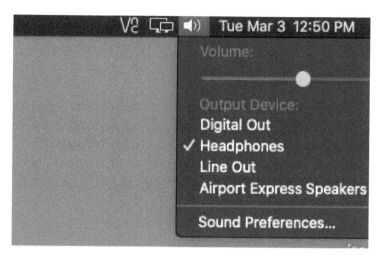

After plugging my headphones into my Airport Express speaker port and placing the headphones on my ears ... finally I got to hear sweet, sweet music.

So this appears, at the moment, to be the only way to get AUDIO from OS X running on ESXi 6.7.

With that being accomplished, you now have a working Mojave or Catalina OS X system running Xcode and being able to produce audio!

Wireless Connection to your iPhone from Xcode

When you configure your Xcode to work with your iPhone/iPad be sure to click the button for 'wireless connectivity'. The next time I ran Xcode I was able to see "my iPhone" in the Xcode target dropdown, and new builds are sent directly to my iPhone wirelessly.

Enjoy!

Chapter 11

BONUS - OTHER RESOURCES

While I can not guarantee a response to every e-mail or request for information, if you have applied one or more of ideas mentioned in this book, "NetScaler Hacks" and want to share that with me, please do so at the email address below.

contact me: admin@n90x.info

In addition, any updates to this book I will post on my website
https://www.n90x.info

Be sure to subscribe to my YouTube channel for video updates (100% Free): https://www.youtube.com/NetScalerTrainer

CRACKING THE NETSCALER PASSWORD

```
BTX loader 1.00  BTX version is 1.02
Consoles: internal video/keyboard
BIOS drive A: is disk0
BIOS drive C: is disk1
BIOS 639kB/2096064kB available memory

FreeBSD/x86 bootstrap loader, Revision NS1.2
Loading /boot/defaults/loader.conf
/ns-11.1-51.21 text=0xb96092 data=0x16f91d68+0x6d7298 syms=[0x8+0xccba0+0x8+0xbd
558]

Press [Ctrl-C] for command prompt, or any other key to boot immediately.
Booting [/ns-11.1-51.21] in 1 second...

Type '?' for a list of commands, 'help' for more detailed help.
OK
```

When Ctrl-C does not work

A client of mine bought 2 NetScaler 5500's on eBay. They both came with the CF and data drives. For some reason he could not communicate with the NetScaler via the serial port to reset the password. Following my suggestions he did the following:

He removed the plastic covering the video port, connected a monitor and keyboard. Then he got into the system BIOS. He discovered the Serial Port was active, but he still could not get Control-C to work from the keyboard. The serial port still refused to connect.

It turns out that NetScalers use an internal hardcoded encryption key for all their devices.

He pulled the CF drive from the NetScaler, connected it to a USB reader and connected this to his PC. He then used **UFS Explorer Professional Recovery** software to read the CF card. He found the **ns.conf** file and opened it. He copied the **nsroot** line with the encrypted password from this configuration file to his PC. He then used a python script to de-encrypt it. Here's a few links to what helped us get there...

FROM: https://dozer.nz/citrix-decrypt/

"Citrix Netscaler (or whatever they're calling it now) uses hardcoded encryption keys to encrypt at least some passwords stored in the appliance config, most importantly for LDAP bind passwords. As a side note - the passwords for accessing the appliance itself via CLI or GUI are hashed, not encrypted. You can still attempt to break these using hashcat but it requires bruteforcing.

However, some other values in the config like LDAP bind passwords are encrypted and can be recovered as by default they are encrypted by hardcoded keys that seem to be common to all Netscalers. These static encryption keys are compliled into the libnscli90.so library on the appliance. As of 10.5 this was the RC4 key 2286da6ca015bcd9b7259753c2a5fbc2. At some point Citrix changed the default key and cipher used to encrypt cleartext values. The default key is now 351CBE38F041320F22D990AD8365889C7DE2FCCCAE5A1A8707E21E and the appliance now (12.0) uses AES256-CBC instead of RC4. I figured out after a quick bit of RE that the version signifier seems the be the -encryptmethod flag, where ENCMTHD_3 signifies it is using AES256-CBC and the new default key."

You need this crypto library to make the **dozer.nz** python script work
https://pycryptodome.readthedocs.io/en/latest/src/installation.html

Other Tools Used:

UFS Explorer Professional Recovery (Windows, OS X and Linux versions are available) https://www.ufsexplorer.com/ufs-explorer-professional-recovery.php

IPMI - LIGHTS OUT MANAGMENT

```
                    BIOS SETUP UTILITY
 Main    Advanced    Security    Boot    Exit
┌─────────────────────────────────────────┬─────────────────────┐
│ Advanced Settings                         │ IPMI configuration  │
│ ─────────────────────────────────────    │ including server    │
│ WARNING: Setting wrong values in below    │ monitoring and      │
│          sections                         │ event log.          │
│       may cause system to malfunction.    │                     │
│                                           │                     │
│ ▶ Boot Features                           │                     │
│ ▶ Processor & Clock Options               │                     │
│ ▶ Advanced Chipset Control                │                     │
│ ▶ I/O Virtualization                      │                     │
│ ▶ IDE/SATA Configuration                  │                     │
│ ▶ PCI/PnP Configuration                   │                     │
│ ▶ SuperIO Configuration                   │                     │
│ ▶ Remote Access Configuration             │  ←    Select Screen │
│ ▶ System Health Monitor                   │  ↑↓   Select Item   │
│ ▶ ACPI Configuration                      │ Enter Go to Sub Screen│
│ ▶ IPMI Configuration                      │ F1    General Help  │
│ ▶ DMI Event Logging                       │ F10   Save and Exit │
│                                           │ ESC   Exit          │
└─────────────────────────────────────────┴─────────────────────┘
       v02.61 (C)Copyright 1985-2006, American Megatrends, Inc.
```

   Those NetScalers with IPMI (Intelligent Platform Management Interface) also know has LOM (Lights Of Management) include the 2nd generation of MPX/SDX units like the MPX/SDX 8200 and 11500. Java is required. I am using Java 7 for my lab as the security requirements are less then Java 8+.

Configure IPMI IP address in BIOS

```
                    BIOS SETUP UTILITY
   Advanced

   IP Address Configuration.                        Options

   Parameter Selector          [03]              Static
   IP Address Source           [Static]          DHCP
   IP Address                  [010.010.010.233]
   Current IP address in BMC:   010.010.010.233




                                              ←    Select Screen
                                              ↑↓   Select Item
                                              +-   Change Option
                                              F1   General Help
                                              F10  Save and Exit
                                              ESC  Exit

        v02.61 (C)Copyright 1985-2006, American Megatrends, Inc.
```

In BIOS you will configured the IP address and netmask. It is
recommended you use a static address.

93

```
                    BIOS SETUP UTILITY
   Advanced

   Subnet Mask Configuration.                    Enter Subnet Mask in
                                                  decimal in the form of
   Parameter Selector          [06]              XXX.XXX.XXX.XXX
   Subnet Mask                 [255.255.255.000] (XXX less than 256
   Current Subnet Mask in BMC:  255.255.255.000   and in decimal only).




                                                  ←    Select Screen
                                                  ↑↓   Select Item
                                                  F1   General Help
                                                  F10  Save and Exit
                                                  ESC  Exit




            v02.61 (C)Copyright 1985-2006, American Megatrends, Inc.
```

Now Save BIOS settings and the system will reboot and initialize the IPMI.

Once IPMI is configured you can connect to your IPMI port and remote control the server from a browser. Functions such as POWER ON / OFF/ RESET as well as console view and remote control are now available.

Connect to IPMI via browser

Now, enter the IP address you configured in a browser. Firefox and Chrome are recommended.

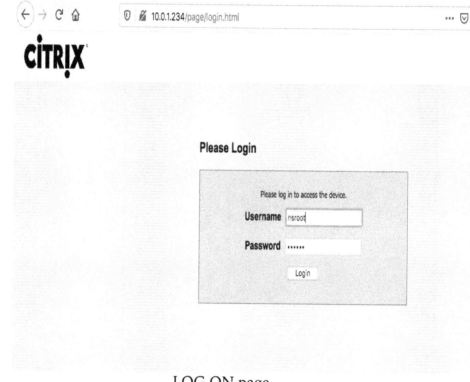

LOG ON page
(default username/password is usually nsroot/nsroot)

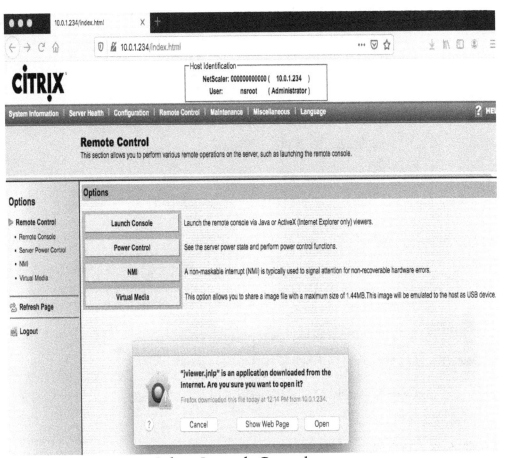

Select Launch Console

Do you want to run this application?

Name: **com.ami.kvm.jviewer.JViewer**

Publisher: UNKNOWN

Locations: http://10.0.1.234

Launched from downloaded JNLP file

Running this application may be a security risk

Risk: This application will run with unrestricted access which may put your computer and personal information at risk. The information provided is unreliable or unknown so it is recommended not to run this application unless you are familiar with its source

More Information

Select the box below, then click Run to start the application

☑ I accept the risk and want to run this application.   Run   Cancel

Accept the risk and click RUN

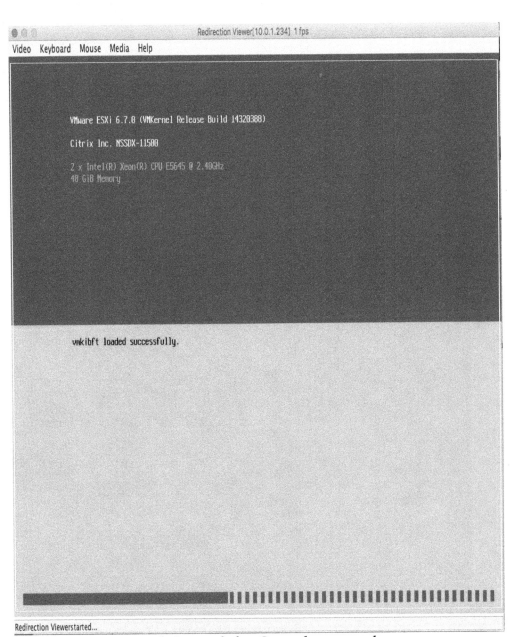

View and Control the Console remotely

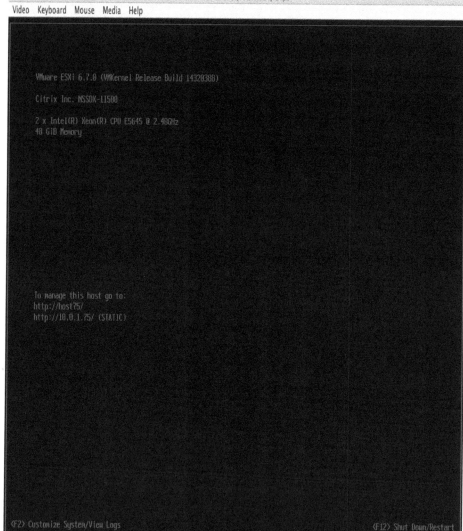

Now you can interact with the NetScaler as if you had a keyboard and monitor directly attached.

SSL Certificates

Best practice is to generate a SSL key pair and secure traffic to the

IPMI port, but for your lab this set up is perfectly fine.

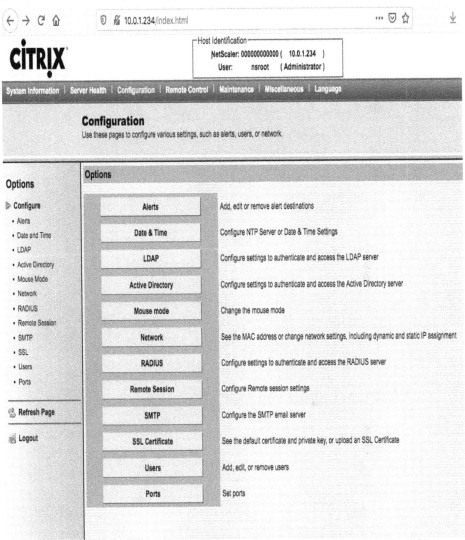

From the IPMI login you can select CONFIGURATION -> SSL
Certificates

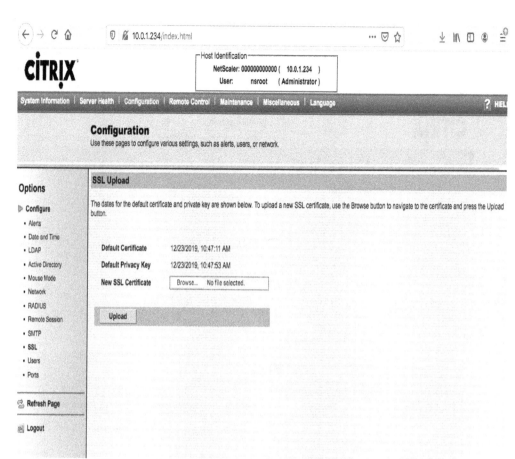

Then upload your SSL Certificates here

VMWARE ESXI HICKUPS

```
                         Loading VMware ESXi
ing /net_nlx4.v01
ing /net_nx_n.v00
ing /net_tg3.v00
ing /net_vmxn.v00
ing /ohci_usb.v00
ing /qlnative.v00
ing /rste.v00
ing /sata_ahc.v00
ing /sata_ata.v00
ing /sata_sat.v00
ing /sata_sat.v01
ing /sata_sat.v02
ing /sata_sat.v03
ing /sata_sat.v04
ing /scsi_aac.v00
ing /scsi_adp.v00
ing /scsi_aic.v00
ing /scsi_bnx.v00
ing /scsi_bnx.v01
ing /scsi_fni.v00
ing /scsi_hps.v00
ing /scsi_ips.v00
ing /scsi_lpf.v00
ing /scsi_meg.v00
ing /scsi_meg.v01
ing /scsi_meg.v02
ing /scsi_mpt.v00
ing /scsi_mpt.v01
ing /scsi_mpt.v02
ing /scsi_qla.v00
ing /scsi_qla.v01
ing /uhci_usb.v00
ing /xorg.v00
ing /imgdb.tgz
ing /state.tgz
ating modules and starting up the kernel...
```

When installing VMware ESXi on NetScaler hardware, if you should seem to get stuck on the screen "**relocating modules and starting the kernel...**" there is a simple fix for this.

reboot the machine

On the start up screen press **SHIFT+O** (shift and letter O)

append "**ignoreHeadless=TRUE**" to the end of the boot options
line

press **enter** to continue the boot process

After your initial ESXi install is complete an automatic reboot will
happen, so apply steps 2) & 3) again to boot up

Enable **SSH** and SSH into the ESXi host

Type the following VMkernel boot-time parameters to make these settings permanent **"esxcfg-advcfg -k TRUE ignoreHeadless"**

Now, after this fix your ESXi host will boot normally.

Chapter 12

FINAL THOUGHTS

Thank You Again For Reading This Book

I hope it inspires you to create something amazing!

I hope you will breath new life into your legacy NetScaler hardware!

I hope you have a lot of fun doing it!

Best regards,

Joseph Moses
Author and Consultant
admin@n90x.info

www.ingramcontent.com/pod-product-compliance
Lightning Source LLC
Chambersburg PA
CBHW031244050326
40690CB00007B/942